Dino Dan

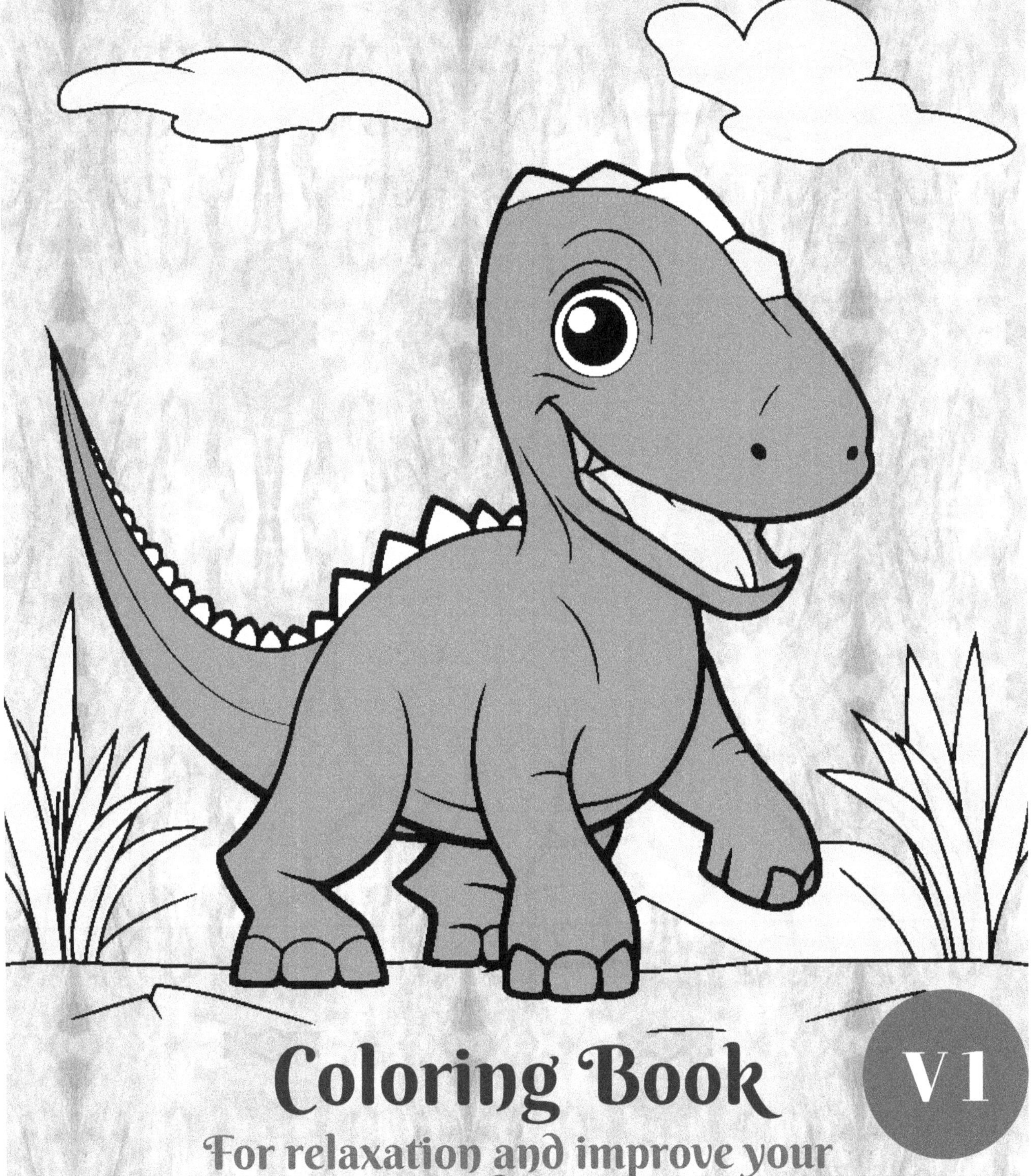

Coloring Book

V1

For relaxation and improve your
attention and concentration

Dino Dan

Coloring Book

This book belongs to: ___________

Dinosaurs

Dinosaurs were a group of reptiles that inhabited the Earth in the Mesozoic era, from the Upper Triassic period to the end of the Cretaceous period (245 to 65 million years ago). Its disappearance marks the limit between the Mesozoic and Cenozoic eras, and the beginning of the so-called age of mammals. The term dinosaur comes from the Greek (it means "terrible lizard") and refers to the most diverse specimens: large, like the brontosaurus, which weighed about 75 tons, and very small, like the Saltopus, only 50 cm long. long.

The first hominids, for their part, appeared on Earth relatively recently, around 2 million years ago, long after the last of these large reptiles perished. The images of the first men next to the dinosaurs are nothing more than a product of fantasy.

COLOR PALETTE

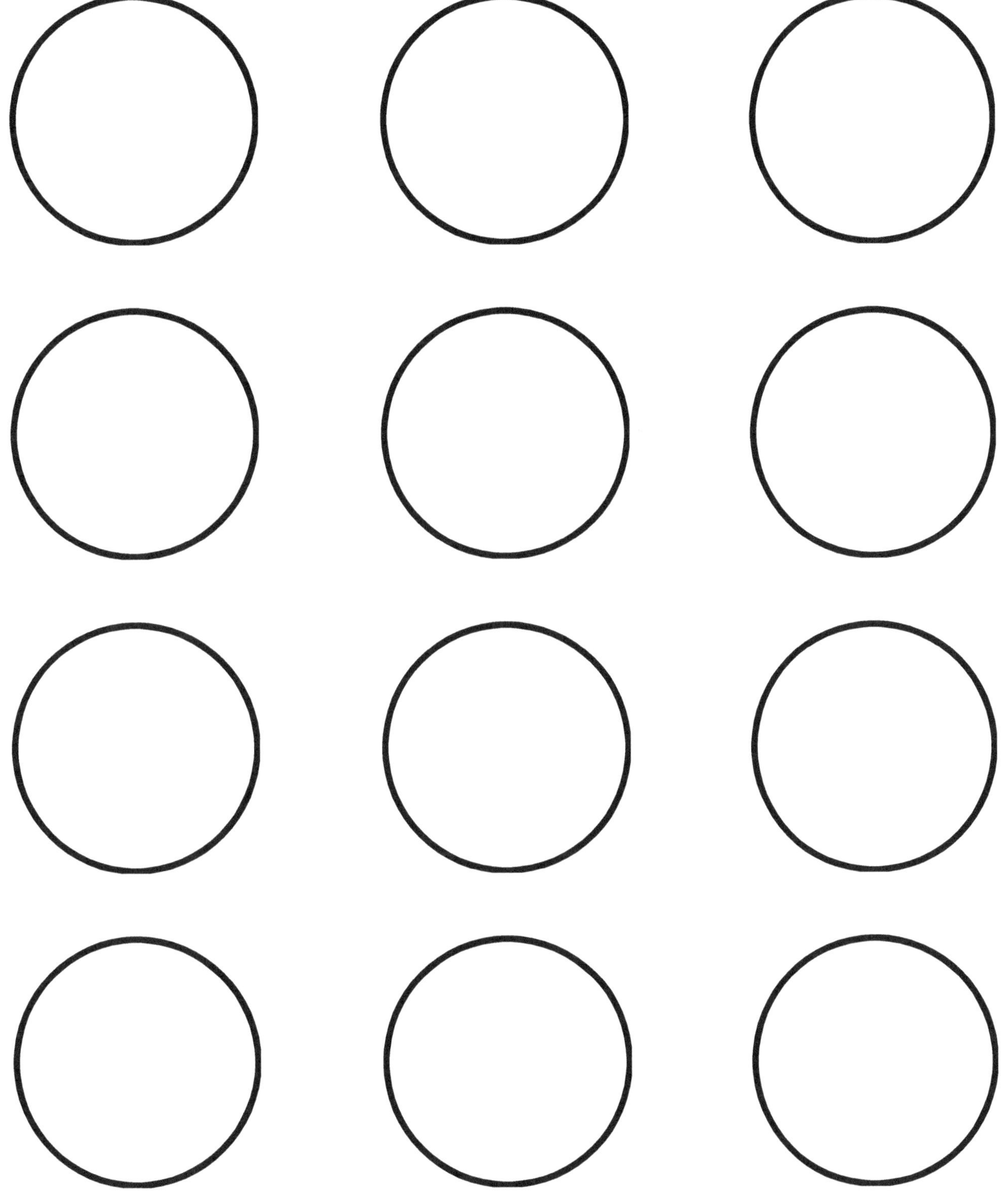

Mordelon

Never stop believing in yourself.

Seekersaurus

Your potential is infinite.

Prodino

Every mistake is an opportunity to learn.

Tenderness

You are the architect of your own destiny.

Cabadino

With effort and perseverance, everything is possible.

Happiness

There are no limits to what you can achieve.

Eater

The magic is within you.

Double Tail

Today is the perfect day to start.

Ferosillo

Your smile lights up the world.

Dino Pony

Be brave and face your fears.

DINO LAUGHTER

Success starts with a dream.

CURIOUS DINO

You are stronger than you think.

BOGGED DINO

If you can dream it, you can achieve it.

TORTU DINA

Determination is the key to success.

SINGING DINO

Your actions define who you are.

SERIOUS DINO

Your actions define who you are.

PLAYFUL DINO

Every step brings you closer to your goals.

DINO FAMILY

You are the hero of your own story.

DINO SPECIAL READER

There are no failures, only lessons.

DINO MANDALA

Hard work always pays off.

FRIENDS

Perseverance overcomes any obstacle.

CUTE DINO

Trust your intuition.

DINO AND THE FUNGUS

You are capable of shining on your own.

FLYING DINO

Never underestimate the power of your dreams.

UNIQUE AND SPECIAL DINOS

Make each day a little better than the last.

DADDY DINO

Your attitude determines your altitude.

DINO STAR

Imagination knows no bounds.

DINO BALLOON

Be kind always, even when it's hard.

BABY DINO

Patience is a virtue

DINO STUDY

Don't give up, success is closer than you think.

LAUGHING DINO

Love and kindness are your superpowers.

DINO SHELL

Every challenge is an opportunity for growth.

CUTE DINO BABY

You are unique and special.

DINO WALKER

You control your emotions.

CHARISMATIC DINO

Curiosity leads to great discoveries.

CRAWLING DINO

Life is a journey, enjoy the ride.

DINO WALKER

Believe in yourself and anything is possible.

DINO GRUMPY MOM

Friendship is an invaluable treasure.

DINA ATTENTIVE BABY

Gratitude turns the ordinary into extraordinary.

TENDER DINA

"You can make a difference in the world.

HAPPY DINO FAMILY

Learn from your mistakes and keep moving forward.

DINO CHASER

Respect is the foundation of all relationships.

SLEEPY DINO

Do good without looking at whom.

CLUELESS DINO

Honesty is always the best policy.

GRUMPY DINO DADDY

Sow good deeds and you will reap great results.

BULLY DINO

Perseverance is the key to success.

FAMILY TRIO

The best way to predict the future is to create it.

CRAZY AND HAPPY DINO FAMILY

You are stronger than you imagine.

DEFENDER MOM

Every day is a new opportunity to be better.

CURIOUS DINO

Self-confidence will take you far.

Q Q E K C Y T D Y S X O T B W

N L S O V I T I S O P C A P S

V S T F E C R O R R C D L E B

J O R O T A V E R O V O V R T

U T I E N R G T S S M Ñ U S E

K N U N E I Ñ X J P J A J E X

N E N T M Ñ X R O Z E U N V I

F I F R C O D C E K Z T F E T

M M O E C R P U L D S I O R O

I A X G F Z R Q T T O K C A V

Y S P A V P Z L D I Y P J N F

N N L U X F D Y R H T K D C M

Q E N T U S I A S M O A W I L

N P U P E D L I M U H W R A X

E E O S I M O R P M O C M G S

AMOR	POSITIVOS	EXITO
CARIÑO	RESPETO	TRIUNFO
ENTUSIASMO	COMPROMISO	PODER
GRATITUD	PERSEVERANCIA	MENTE
PENSAMIENTOS	ENTREGA	HUMILDE